CW00471262

For my parents,
Paul and Lin Daniels who taught me
from an early age to seek God
and his wisdom.

Introduction

When I was baptised at the age of eleven years, my grandparents gifted me with an NIV Bible. I still have that Bible and in the front of it they quoted Proverbs 3:5-6:

> Trust in the Lord with all your heart
> and lean not on your own understanding;
> in all your ways submit to him,
> and he will make your paths straight.

Over time, these two verses have become my life verses. They are a key part of my life and mean so much to me. God regularly brings them to my remembrance.

Proverbs is such a great book for teaching us spiritual wisdom, for giving us guidance, insight and direction.

I recently read through the book of Proverbs in my Quiet Time with God and shared my #prayingthroughproverbs on social media. People liked and commented on them and so I decided to produce this book of prayers and make it available to more people.

There are a variety of ways you can read this book. You may decide to read a prayer a day for a month or you may like to use it in your own Quiet Time, first reading the proverb for yourself, asking God to reveal his truth to you personally for that day, finishing by reading the prayer I have written. You may also like to write in your journal (if you keep one) your own prayer based on the Proverb you have read.

Proverbs 1

Lord God,

How I need your godly wisdom on a moment by moment, day to day basis. Choosing to worship you and submitting to your will for me is the starting point to wisdom. Please keep me from being unteachable or over-confident in my own wisdom.

Amen

Proverbs 2

Lord God,

As I look over my day there is so much I feel needs to be done and many who rely on me. I don't know where to start and I don't know what to say to those who need my support and encouragement. So, I'm coming before you now to listen to your words of wisdom. I ask for a heart of understanding; for knowledge and insight to make wise choices and for the words to speak into the lives of others.

Amen

Proverbs 3

Lord God,

Sometimes I think I know what's best for myself and those I care about, and I lean on my own understanding. But when I do this, things end up in a mess. Life is so much better when I choose to trust you with all my heart. You are Lord of my life and I surrender my will to yours. When I submit to you, I sense you directing me and guiding me along the right path and this brings me joy and peace.

Amen

Proverbs 4

Lord God,

It may be easier to go along with the crowd, but that doesn't make it right. So, I'm coming to you at the start of this new day to listen carefully and pay attention to your instructions. I'm meditating on your word and taking them to heart. Then when a choice is before me, I will know the way to take. As I fix my eyes ahead, your light shines before me and nothing will hold me back.

Amen

Proverbs 5

Lord God,

Thank you for watching over my life. You watch over me, not waiting to condemn me when I fail, but to show your love for me and encourage me. Help me to keep far away from any situation I know will cause me to be tempted and give me strength to overcome.

Amen

Proverbs 6

Lord God,

I thank you for my parents who taught me from an early age to love and follow you. Thank you for mature Christians you have brought into my life who give me wise counsel and advice. Thank you too for your Holy Spirit who is my counsellor and instructs me in the way I should go. Thank you that when it comes to making decisions, I have people I can go to for guidance and who will help me to think more objectively. May I be the kind of person others will seek out when they too have a decision to make because they know I will give them godly advice.

Amen

Proverbs 7

Lord God,

Your word is my most treasured possession. As I meditate on it would you help me to commit it to memory. May my love for your word translate into action. I know that hiding your word in my heart and obeying it will guard me from sin.

Amen

Proverbs 8

Lord God,

I desire the wisdom that comes from you. Nothing on earth can compare with it. Please give me an open and willing mind to hear your words of wisdom. There are many areas in which you call me to lead - at home, work and church - and it's your wisdom which helps me to lead in a godly way.

Amen

Proverbs 9

Lord God,

I'm feasting on your word this morning. Thank you for the invitation to sit and learn from you. Would you give me spiritual instruction for today that I might walk with spiritual insight and understanding. Where I need correction may I humbly receive and accept it from you.

Amen

Proverbs 10

Lord God,

Help me to apply wisdom to the words I use. May I store up and treasure your wisdom in my heart so when I speak my words are valuable, life-giving and a source of blessing. May my words be encouraging and helpful. May they bring peace and unity rather than causing arguments to escalate. Help me remember that sometimes it is wiser to keep silent. May my motivation in speaking never be about needing to hear the sound of my own voice or trying to appear wiser than I am. Help me discern when words are needed and when it is better to be quiet.

Amen

Proverbs 11

Lord God,

Please help me to live a life worthy of the calling I have received from you. May I always walk humbly before you. May I be known for being honest and trustworthy. Thank you for all the ways you have generously blessed and refreshed me. May I generously share that blessing and refreshment with others.

Amen

Proverbs 12

Lord God,

No discipline is pleasant, but I recognise that when you discipline me you always do it out of love for me and to make me more like Jesus. Help me to have the wisdom to accept it because I know it strengthens my faith and draws me closer to you.

Amen

Proverbs 13

Lord God,

Would you give me the wisdom to think before I act. When I'm tempted to run ahead of you or follow my own plans may I take the time to consider my actions and what the consequences might be. May I make time to talk it through with you and other wise people before I take action.

Amen

Proverbs 14

Lord God,

When I've kept anger buried in my heart it made me physically ill. Holding on to anger, jealousy, unforgiveness and bitterness has a negative impact on my spiritual, emotional and physical wellbeing. Instead may I store up in my heart peace, joy, contentment and love. Then I will experience wellbeing deep within my soul.

Amen

Ii Jj Kk Ll Mm Nn Oo Pp Qq Rr Ss Tt Uu Vv Ww
Grade 2
Public School
Arithmetic (Math)
Singing
Science
Social Studies
Spelling
Do Not Erase
or write on boards
"Museum Rules"
The Teachers
Patterns in Arithmetic 3

Proverbs 15

Lord God,

I hunger after wisdom and understanding. May I learn from those who are wiser than me. Help me to accept with humility, any constructive criticism, correction or advice I am given. Help me to discern what I need to pay attention to and what I need to let go of. Thank you, Lord, for listening to my prayer.

Amen

Proverbs 16

Lord God,

I have plans, hopes and dreams for my life but I bring them all before you. I surrender them to you, trusting you because in your wisdom you know what is right and best for me. Would you grow the dream you have planted within me. Direct my steps and guide me, I pray.

Amen

Proverbs 17

Lord God,

Help me not to hold grudges when those closest to me offend me. May I not dwell on the offence and allow unforgiveness or bitterness to take root. May I not bring up past offences or keep a record of wrongs. Help me to forgive and respond with love, doing all I can to restore the relationship.

Amen

Proverbs 18

Lord God,

I thank you for being my friend. Thank you for always being there for me whatever happens. Thank you that you pursued a relationship with me and that you continue to pursue me. Thank you for being a tower of strength. I know I can run straight into your heart and you will keep me safe.

Amen

Proverbs 19

Lord God,

As a young person I had ideas concerning your plan for my life. But I realise now I misunderstood what your plan was. It is only now as I look back I understand it better. I give you thanks that it is your plan which will succeed, and I ask you to continue revealing your purpose to me.

Amen

Proverbs 20

Lord God,

Thank you for being the one who directs my life and shows me the steps to take. I don't know exactly what my future holds as you only reveal to me one step at a time. But today I'm choosing to step out in faith. I am following your counsel and the advice of godly people you have brought into my life.

Amen

Proverbs 21

Lord God,

My desire is to live a life which is pleasing to you. Would you examine my heart and motives. Show me when I am motivated more by making a name for myself, when I am seeking approval from others or motivated by any other selfish reasons. May my motives spring from a pure and godly heart seeking to bring glory to your name.

Amen

Proverbs 22

Lord God,

May I listen carefully to your words. May they become the guiding principles for my life. May I store your wisdom, instruction and truth in my heart. Help me to pass on to others what I have learned so I can guide, strengthen and bless them too.

Amen

Proverbs 23

Lord God,

Rather than envying the lives others have, may my life be taken up with reverently fearing and worshipping you. Help me to remember in you I have a future and a hope. May I listen to you to receive wisdom, instruction and understanding. Then I know the direction I'm to take in life.

Amen

Proverbs 24

Lord God,

Just as honey is good for me and sweet to taste, so is your wisdom good for my life and sweet to my soul. Help me to digest your word so it becomes a part of me and flows out through me. Living out your wisdom brings me a future and a hope which endures and does not disappoint.

Amen

Proverbs 25

Lord God,

I treasure the words of advice you have given me from the mouths of others. They have come at just the right time in just the right way. They have been such a blessing. Help me to also humbly listen to constructive criticism given by a spiritually wise person and to accept there is value in it and something to be learned from it.

Amen

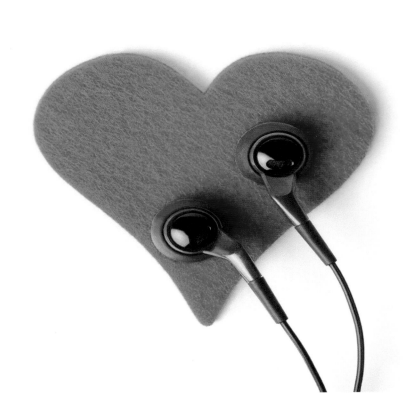

Proverbs 26

Lord God,

Please help me to learn from my mistakes and not keep repeating them. May I always be teachable and humble rather than think I know it all. May I be attentive to what is happening around me and make the most of every opportunity. May I be careful with my words; may I never add fuel to the fire by gossiping or lying; may no deceit or anger be found in my heart.

Amen

Proverbs 27

Lord God,

Help me to be a good and wise friend. One who speaks the truth in love and gives wise advice. May I be someone who walks alongside my friend in their Christian journey, encouraging them to mature in their faith and follow God's will. Supporting them when the going is tough, rather than abandoning them when they need me the most.

Amen

Proverbs 28

Lord God,

I recognise your word is true and right. May I never turn my back on your teaching. When I seek you, I have a better understanding and appreciation for your word. I trust and rely on your word. May I never close my heart and refuse to listen to you. Thank you that if I sin against you and your word, I just need to confess and turn from my sin and I will receive compassion, mercy and forgiveness.

Amen

Proverbs 29

Lord God,

There is joy and blessing in obeying your word. Please give me a fresh revelation of yourself and your will for my life. I trust you and am putting my confidence in you rather than allowing fear of others have any control over the way I live my life.

Amen

Proverbs 30

Lord God,

I will continue to seek to know you all my days. I want to grow in my knowledge of you, not just in my head but in my heart too. You are the source of wisdom. Your word is true and pure. You are a faithful God, I trust in you and take refuge in you.

Amen

Proverbs 31

Lord God,

Thank you that I am worth more to you than any precious jewel. I am precious in your sight. With all that I am, I worship, obey, serve and trust you. The future holds no fear for me because you are holding me.

Amen

About the Author

I live in Eastbourne, in the South East of England, with my husband, Jason, and my two adult children, Josh and Jess.

We attend Gateway Christian Church where my husband is the Associate Minister and I am on the Preaching/Teaching Team.

God has blessed me with a love for His Word, for studying it and for sharing His Word with others. I enjoy teaching from His Word and helping others to see how it relates to their lives in the 21st Century, whether that's on a Sunday morning or weekday event.

If you would like to connect with me, you can do so via:
- Twitter: @vickicotting14
- Facebook: @VickiCottinghamWriter
- Instagram: @VickiCottingham
- www.vickicottingham.com

My other books:
- Dear Friend... Volume 1
- Dear Friend... Volume 2

Each book has 52 weekly devotions to encourage, challenge and inspire and are available from Amazon.

Printed in Poland
by Amazon Fulfillment
Poland Sp. z o.o., Wrocław